DAYS OF SLAVERY

By Stuart Kallen

ABDO
& Daughters

Published by ABDO Publishing Company, 4940 Viking Drive, Edina, MN 55435.
Copyright © 2001 by Abdo Consulting Group, Inc. International copyrights reserved
in all countries. No part of this book may be reproduced in any form without
written permission from the publisher.

Printed in the United States.

Edited by: Paul Joseph
Graphic Design: City Desktop Productions

Cover Photos: Corbis
Interior Photos: Corbis

Library of Congress Cataloging-in-Publication Data

Kallen, Stuart A., 1955-
    Days of Slavery / Stuart Kallen
       p. cm. -- (Black History)
    Includes index.
    Summary:
    ISBN 1-57765-470-6
    1. Slavery--United States--History--Juvenile literature. 2. Afro-
Americans--History--To 1863--Juvenile literature. [1.
Slavery--History. 2. Afro-Americans--History--To 1863.] I. Title.

E441 .K15 2001
973'.0496--dc21

00-056885

CONTENTS

African-American slaves work in the cotton fields of a plantation.

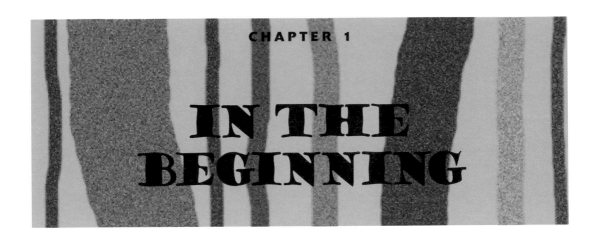

CHAPTER 1

IN THE BEGINNING

Since ancient times, foreigners have exported gold, silver, ivory, and other valuable goods from Africa to the rest of the world. They have also exported the people who lived there. For many centuries, armies from other continents captured African people. These men, women, and children were taken to their conquerors' homelands to become slaves.

Slavery is as old as civilization. Both blacks

An obelisk and a statue of a slave breaking free from his chains commemorate the abolition of slavery.

5

and whites were forced into slavery in ancient Rome and Greece. Europeans used each other as slaves for centuries. In fact, the word "slave" comes from the days when people from Germany sold the Slavs, or Eastern Europeans, as slaves. When the Moslems came to Africa, around 900 A.D., they sold thousands of Africans to Persia and Saudi Arabia. Slavery was also common in Asia.

When the Roman Empire controlled Europe, the Romans used the English as slaves. Tacitus, a Roman historian, complained in the ninth century that the English were not smart enough to make good slaves. Still, the Romans forced them into labor until the eleventh century.

But after being slaves for hundreds of years, the English eventually became the most powerful slave traders of all time. Between 1620 and 1750, the English kidnapped four times as many Africans as all the other European countries combined.

Engraving. *The African Slave Trade.*

Portuguese Slave Traders

The Beginnings of a Lucrative Business

In 1441, Anthony Gonsalves was captain of a ship that sailed down the western coast of Africa. It was a dangerous journey, and his sailors were very daring men. They were 1,700 miles from their homeland, Portugal. Few Europeans had ever visited Africa.

When Gonsalves returned to Portugal, his ship carried 12 Africans that his men captured. Two years later, Gonsalves returned to Africa. Again, he kidnapped native Africans and took them home to Portugal. He sold these people into slavery. Very quickly, the idea of buying and selling African slaves spread throughout Europe.

Capturing Africans and bringing them to Europe was a risky business. The African coast was an unexplored place. Death and disease always lurked nearby. Also, many Europeans thought slavery was immoral. But the slave traders ignored both the protests and the dangers. The demand for human slaves continued to grow. Hundreds of men became slave traders to fill this demand.

The New World

The first blacks that came to America were sailors, not slaves. Some historians believe that a black man traveled to the New World with Christopher Columbus. When Vasco de Balboa discovered the Pacific Ocean in 1513, at least 30 black men sailed with him. Blacks also sailed with Hernán Cortés to Peru and with the French to Canada.

In the early 1500s, a Moroccan man named Estevanico became both a slave and an explorer. Around 1520, he was sold into slavery by Portuguese invaders and sent to Europe. He became the personal servant of a Spanish explorer named Andres de Dorantes. Dorantes

Vasco de Balboa seeing the Pacific Ocean for the first time.

treated Estevanico well, and the two became good friends. In 1527, they joined an expedition that sailed to Florida and then Texas. Out of over 300 sailors, only 80 made it to Texas. Those 80 were enslaved by the natives. Only four survived, including Dorantes and

Estevanico. They escaped in 1534. After their escape, they became famous among friendly Indian tribes as travelers and medicine men. Estevanico learned several Indian languages. He bravely led several expeditions into what is now the American Southwest.

Conquistador Hernán Cortés.

By 1515, the Spanish had a foothold in the New World. The Spaniards began exporting sugar from the West Indies to Europe. But the Arawak Indians, who lived in the West Indies, refused to work for them. So the Spaniards began bringing captured Africans to work in the sugarcane fields. Within a few years, they were importing hundreds and hundreds of African slaves.

In 1619, the first black slaves were brought to America. They worked in the tobacco fields around Jamestown, Virginia. Tobacco was a very profitable crop, and so the slaves who grew tobacco became extremely valuable. The slave trade quickly became a major industry.

The Spanish, Portuguese, French, English, Dutch, and Danish all fought to control the slave trade. Ships from these countries kidnapped more than 80,000 Africans each year. Slave trading companies like the Royal African Company made so much money that they called the Africans "Black Gold."

Eventually, the English won the fight to control the slave trade. By 1713, they were the masters of the sea.

The first black slaves in America were imported to work in the tobacco fields around Jamestown, Virginia.

Back in Africa

The Europeans who favored slavery thought that Africa was a savage and backward place. But Africa had very advanced civilizations and cities. Many Africans lived in societies where they made things from leather, woven cotton, cast iron, and bronze. They grew a wide variety of foods. Some were artists, dancers, and musicians. Others became scholars and teachers. But the slave traders refused to notice these skills and talents. They treated the Africans not as people, but as products to buy and sell, like spices or silk.

To capture slaves, the traders first filled their ships with cloth, liquor, guns, gunpowder, and food. They sailed to Africa, rowed ashore, and set up trading posts. They visited the chief of a nearby

Aerial view of Goree Island, Senegal.

tribe and offered him gifts. The chief would then send his own men to kidnap strangers or members of an enemy tribe. These captives were traded to the Europeans for guns and liquor. Many times, the chiefs had to provide slaves to avoid becoming slaves themselves. Some chiefs became very powerful with the guns they obtained from the slave traders.

Some slave ships made five or six stops before they collected enough slaves. Then the sailors loaded the ships with corn, yams, fruits, beans, coconuts, and water and set sail for America.

Three slave traders throw African slaves overboard into the ocean during the middle passage to America.

Most African slaves that came to America were from Gambia, the Gold Coast, Guinea, or Senegal. The people from Senegal were skilled craftsmen and brought a higher price. The Eboes from Calabar, on the other hand, were considered undesirable. Many Eboes committed suicide to avoid becoming slaves.

One-Way Passage

For a newly captured person, life on a slave ship was horrible. Small sailing vessels were packed with as many as 400 slaves. Slaves cost about $25 in Africa and sold for up to $200 in America. This was a large sum of money in those days. The more Africans the slave traders could fit on their ships, the more money they made.

On the ship, the slaves were chained together at the hands and ankles. Each man was crammed into a space six feet long and 16 inches wide. Women and children were allowed even less space. Everyone lived in filth, and they were poorly fed. The journey across the ocean took anywhere from three weeks to three months. Seasickness and disease took their toll on the prisoners. The groans of dying prisoners filled the air.

Any slave that resisted was tortured. Many chose to jump into the ocean and drown rather than remain prisoners. Historians estimate that one out of every seven slaves died during the passage to America. Sometimes slaves rebelled, took command of a ship, and killed the crew. But sooner or later these rebels were harshly punished.

No one knows exactly how many Africans were brought to America as slaves. Many historians say that Africa lost about 10 million people to the slave trade. While Africans died, the slave trade made thousands of Americans and Europeans very wealthy.

Strangers in a Strange Land

If the slaves survived the ocean crossing, new ordeals awaited them in America. A town crier announced the arrival of the slave ship. Plantation owners came down to the docks to purchase field hands and servants. As they were auctioned off, the half-naked slaves shivered in the new, colder climate.

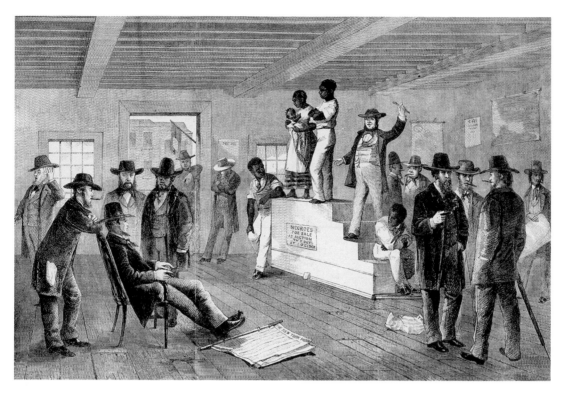

Slave auction

Marriages and families meant nothing to the plantation owners. Husbands were separated from wives, and parents were separated from their children. Most never saw each other again. Indeed, slave owners often separated families on purpose, so they could not join together to plan a rebellion. Family members begged and cried not to be taken from one another. The slave traders ignored their cries.

The slave owners also separated the members of a tribe from one another. Members of different tribes spoke different languages. Because of this, many slaves found themselves stranded. They had no families, did not know the language of the white people, and were not able to talk to the other slaves. These slaves were faced with a lifetime of hard work, no pay, meager food, and the lash of the whip.

Slave woman being dragged by slave trader.

Thousands of field hands were needed to clear the forests for plantations. Thousands more were needed for tending crops such as rice, indigo, cotton, sugar, and tobacco. By 1700, there were twice as many black people as white people in America. Most of them lived on the Southern plantations.

CHAPTER 2

LIVING IN AMERICA

In 1830, a Florida planter bragged that "I work my slaves in a hurrying time until 12 o'clock at night. Then I have 'em up again by four in the morning." This was the life of a slave.

Marching slaves to the fields.

Twenty-hour workdays were the rule, six days a week. Slaves froze in the winter, sweated in the hot summer sun, and got drenched in the rain.

A gong or horn awakened the slaves before dawn. Slave drivers marched them to the fields immediately, and they worked until about 10 a.m. After a meal of hoecake (cornmeal heated on a hoe over an open fire) the slaves worked until late in the afternoon. Then they took another 15-minute break for dinner. The work continued until it was too dark to see. The slaves had to turn in the crops, feed the mules, chop the wood, and attend to the master. Only then did they have time to mend their clothes, eat, drink some water, and relax. Men, women, and children all worked this way. Many received only one blanket, one pair of shoes, and two changes of clothes a year.

Eli Whitney revolutionized the cotton industry with his invention, the cotton gin. He is considered a pioneer of the concept of mass production.

Slaves working on a cotton plantation operate the first cotton gin.

The Cotton Gin

In 1793, Eli Whitney invented a new machine that turned cotton into a major crop. This invention was called the cotton gin. It was operated by a hand crank, and it separated the sticky seeds from the useful cotton fibers. Before Whitney's invention, this work was done by hand. It was a long, slow process. A whole household, including the servants, would gather by the fireplace after dinner. Everybody removed the cotton lint from the seeds, fiber by fiber. In this way, a few pounds of cotton could be gathered before bedtime.

African-American slaves in a cotton field.

By using the cotton gin, one person could remove the seeds from 10 times as much cotton as before. The cotton was placed in a box that had rakelike fingers on each side. A crank was turned and the fingers separated the cotton from the seeds. After a few years, larger models were made that used a horse for power. With these new models, 50 times as much cotton could be seeded each day.

Cotton quickly passed tobacco to become the major crop in the South. Hundreds of thousands of acres of cotton were planted. But to grow cotton, pick it, gin it, and bale it was still very hard work. Slaves did almost all of this work. In 1803, 10 years after the invention of the cotton gin, more than 20,000 Africans were brought to Georgia and South Carolina to work the cotton fields. Most of them were supplied by New England slave traders. Whitney's gin turned cotton into big business. It also brought the chains of slavery even tighter around the ankles of the Africans.

Life on a Plantation

Tobacco and cotton were most profitable when grown on huge areas of land. Plantations of 10,000 acres or more were common during the 1800s. The families who owned plantations lived like kings and queens. Their mansions were filled with Persian rugs, fine artwork, and imported furnishings. Some mansions contained a music room, a library, a ballroom, several parlors, a huge dining room, a kitchen, and a wine cellar. Lavish parties were given for visiting friends and relatives.

Bedroom of plantation manor house

Surrounding many of these mansions were bake houses, stables, dairies, and schoolhouses where teachers lived. Many also had blacksmith shops, brickworks, smokehouses, flour mills, and cabins for slaves. Items that could not be made on the plantation were imported from Europe.

Louisiana Plantation

Skilled Workers

Slaves were important to almost every aspect of the plantation. Not all slaves worked in the fields. Some were skilled craftsmen. They built and repaired houses, barns, roads, bridges, gates, and fences. Many slave owners encouraged their slaves to learn skills. The

A white southern family dines, waited on by African-American servants.

owners could earn money by hiring out skilled slaves to other planters. Slaves became railroad firemen, bricklayers, blacksmiths, printers, carpenters, and more.

House servants were often better off than field hands. Cooks, butlers, nannies, hairdressers, seamstresses, and others served plantation owners and their families. Often the house servants helped raise their owner's children. House servants were sometimes allowed to learn to read and write.

TIMELINE

1441 The Portuguese start the slave trade

1500–1530 Many blacks sail with explorers on expeditions to the new world

1513 Vasco de Balboa discovers the Pacific Ocean

1515 Spanish begin importing captured Africans to work the sugarcane fields of the West Indies

1619 First black slaves brought to America

1700 Blacks outnumber whites in America 2 to 1

1770 Crispus Attucks killed in the Boston Massacre

1775 Revolutionary War begins

1779 Jean DuSable builds the first home in what would become Chicago

1783 Revolutionary War ends, slavery continues

1793 Eli Whitney invents the cotton gin

1803 Louisiana Purchase doubles
the size of the United States

1816 The United States Military
destroys Fort Negro

1817 American Colonization Society
forms to send free blacks back to Africa

CHAPTER 3

CONTRIBUTIONS TO EARLY AMERICA

Many blacks, free and slave, made names for themselves in the early days of America. Black writers, actors, athletes, inventors, and soldiers proved their skills and courage to white society again and again. Here are the stories of just a few of the famous black people in American history.

Crispus Attucks (1723–1770)

Leader in the Revolution

"The first to defy and the first to die." This line of poetry was written about Crispus Attucks, a black sailor. In 1770, a group of Boston men were protesting British policies in America. Crispus Attucks was the first to be shot when the British opened fire on the protesters.

Attucks was a slave in Massachusetts until he was 27 years old. He ran away from his owner and went to sea on a whaling ship. For the next 20 years, Attucks sailed the world, hunting whales. While at sea, he taught himself to read and write. Attucks protected his freedom and longed for the freedom of others. It was natural for him to join the Americans who wanted freedom from the British.

On March 5, 1770, a crowd of people gathered in Boston Commons and began taunting a small group of British soldiers. Crispus Attucks, who was well known as an opponent of British rule, was in the crowd. A soldier named Huge Montgomery hit a small boy on the head with his rifle butt. Led by Attucks, the angry crowd began pelting Montgomery with ice and snowballs. Twelve British soldiers came to Montgomery's aid with their rifles and bayonets at the ready.

Attucks charged ahead with a large stick. He yelled, "Don't be afraid. Knock 'em over. They dare not fire." But Attucks was wrong.

Boston Massacre

The soldiers fired, killing him immediately. Nine other men were wounded, and four of them died. Newspapers all over the country called the attack the Boston Massacre.

Attucks' body lay in state in Boston's Faneuil Hall for three days. Thousands attended his funeral. Shopkeepers closed their stores to protest his death. The Boston Massacre was a turning point in American history. It marked the beginning of a series of events that led to the American Revolution.

Jean DuSable (1745–1818)

Founder of Chicago

Jean DuSable was born in Haiti to an African woman and a French man. When Jean was young, his father took him to France to be educated. When he was older, DuSable went to New Orleans to become a fur trapper.

After he left New Orleans, DuSable traveled to a place the Native Americans called "Checagou." DuSable thought it would be a good place to set up a trading post. By 1779, he had built the first permanent home on the northern bank of what is now the Chicago River. The settlement grew and was eventually renamed Chicago. Today it is the third-largest city in America.

DuSable was successful because he could speak English, French, Spanish, and several Native American dialects. He also became friends with the Native American tribes in the area and traded furs with them. Before long, DuSable's post included a horse stable, workshop, bakery, dairy, smokehouse, and other buildings. It became the main supply station for hundreds of fur trappers, traders, and Indians.

DuSable was not honored in his lifetime, but in 1968, he finally received credit for being the founding father of Chicago.

Skyscrapers near the Chicago River in present day Chicago.

Benjamin Banneker (1731–1806)

Inventor and Astronomer

"The color of the skin is in no way connected with the strength of the mind or intellectual powers." So said Benjamin Banneker, a genius of incredible powers.

Benjamin Banneker was born on a farm near Baltimore, Maryland, in 1731. He went to a Quaker school in the wintertime. He was taught to read and write and showed a strong interest in math at a young age.

When Benjamin was 19, he met a traveling salesman who showed him a pocket watch. Banneker had never seen one before, and he went home and drew up plans to make one. He carved the entire watch out of wood and made each gear by hand. His homemade watch kept perfect time for 40 years. It was the first watch made in America.

Banneker studied the stars, and predicted a solar eclipse on April 14, 1789. Many astronomers disagreed with him, but he was correct. Banneker published an almanac listing weather information, eclipses, tide tables, and the hours of sunrises and sunsets. In addition, he published antislavery poems and essays.

When Thomas Jefferson said that blacks were not as smart as whites, Banneker wrote him a letter of protest. He also sent Jefferson a copy of his almanac, and Jefferson quickly changed his mind. Banneker's almanac was later shown in Britain's Parliament and the Academy of Sciences in Paris.

Thomas Jefferson

In 1790, President George Washington asked Banneker to help build the nation's capital. Banneker became part of a three-man team that chose the sites for the White House, the Capitol, and other federal buildings. Banneker also proposed that the United States government establish a Department of Peace, give free education to everyone, and eliminate the death penalty. In many ways, he was a man ahead of his time.

United States Capitol building, Washington, D.C.

Peter Salem (1750–1816)

Revolutionary War Soldier

Because the Declaration of Independence said, "All men are created equal," many black soldiers signed up to fight for the Revolutionary

Army. But many whites did not want blacks to fight. George Washington ordered all black men to leave the army. After he did this, the British offered freedom to any slave who joined their army. Many slaves tried to do so. Washington quickly realized that this would give the British a large advantage. He decided to allow slaves to join his troops. As soon as he did, Peter Salem, a black man, joined the Revolution.

In June 1775, during an early battle in the Revolutionary War, 1,500 American soldiers faced over 2,500 British soldiers in the Battle of Bunker Hill. The British charged up the hill again and again, but the Americans fought them off. When the British thought they were about to win the battle, their commander, Major John Pitcairn, yelled, "The day is ours!" As soon as he spoke, he was shot in the chest by Peter Salem. Pitcairn was one of the best British majors, and his death was a great blow to the British.

The Battle of Bunker Hill.

Many blacks thought that slavery would be abolished if the Americans won. Five thousand blacks served in the Revolutionary Army. Blacks fought in every battle of the eight-year war.

Peter Salem fought bravely at Concord, Lexington, Bunker Hill, Stoney Point, and Saratoga. But blacks were not helped much by the Revolutionary War. After the Americans won, many black soldiers gained their freedom, but others were forced to become slaves again. Salem died in a poorhouse in 1816.

Paul Cuffe (1759–1817)

Shipping Merchant and Humanitarian

Paul Cuffe believed that blacks could only be free if they returned to Africa. He is considered the father of the Black Back-to-Africa movement.

Cuffe was born on Cuttyhunk Island in Massachusetts. His father was a former slave and his mother was a Wampanoag Indian. When he was 16 years old, Cuffe went to sea on a whaling ship. Eventually, he became wealthy from shipping, fishing, and whaling. He owned many ships that sailed to Europe, Africa, Canada, and the Caribbean. He employed many black sailors.

Cuffe's wealth, however, could not protect him from discrimination. The 1778 Massachusetts Constitution denied blacks and Native Americans the right to vote. Because of this, Cuffe refused to pay his taxes. He pointed out to the Massachusetts lawmakers that many blacks and Native Americans were fighting in the American Revolution. He argued that if these people were willing to die for American freedom, they should also be able to vote. The lawmakers finally agreed. In 1783, they granted all taxpaying blacks the right to vote.

When the state would not provide free education to the children in his town, Cuffe built a schoolhouse on his own farm and donated it to the city of Westport.

When the leaders of the hard-won American Revolution refused to end slavery, Cuffe looked to Africa for freedom. In 1810, he traveled to Sierra Leone, in Africa, with the idea of setting up a colony for American blacks. In 1815, Cuffe paid for 20 children and 18 adults to settle with him in Africa.

At the same time that Cuffe was setting up an Afro-American colony, the American Colonization Society was formed. Its leaders were slaveholders. They wanted to send free blacks to Africa so that they would not influence the slaves. The American Congress agreed with the slaveholders. Congress bought territory in Africa where blacks could settle. The country was called Liberia (after the word "Liberty") and its capital was named Monrovia after President James Monroe.

African-American refugees awaiting transportation to Liberia.

Over the next 30 years, more than 14,000 black people returned to Africa. Some were free blacks. Others were slaves who were freed under the condition that they return to Africa. Many blacks would not leave America. They wanted to fight for freedom for the millions of blacks living there. They believed that because blacks helped build America, they were entitled to the same benefits that America offered white people.

York (1770–1832)

Explorer

In 1803, President Thomas Jefferson bought 828,000 square miles of unexplored territory from France. Stretching from Canada to Mexico and from the Mississippi River to the Rocky Mountains, the Louisiana Purchase doubled the size of the United States overnight.

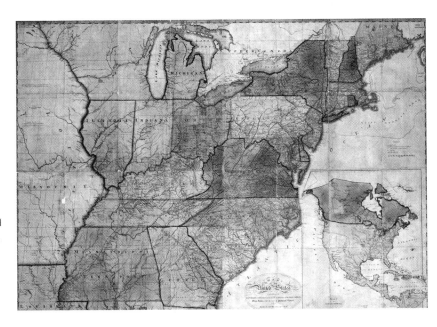

Map of the United States in 1804 soon after the Louisiana Purchase.

Soldiers in the Place d'armer in New Orleans raise an American flag and fire a salute during ceremonies in which Louisiana was transferred from Spain and France to the United States.

No one knew what lay in the vast territories. To find out, Congress sent Meriwether Lewis and William Clark to explore the area. Jefferson also wanted Lewis and Clark to find a route to the Pacific Ocean.

In 1804, the Lewis and Clark expedition set out for the wilderness. Among the 46 people in the party was a black man named York. York was the personal slave of William Clark. The two had been friends since childhood. The 23-year-old York was an imposing figure. He stood over six feet tall and weighed more than 200 pounds. He was an agile hunter, strong and athletic. He spoke French and several Native American dialects.

A French trapper guided the expedition. His wife, Sacajawea, was a Shoshone Indian. When the expedition met with other Native American tribes, Sacajawea told her husband what they were saying. Carbonneau would tell York in French, and York would translate it into English for William Clark. York's translations were very important to the expedition.

The Native Americans were amazed by York. They had never seen a man of his size, skin color, and ability. They thought his face was painted with charcoal, because Native American warriors sometimes painted their faces that way. The Native Americans tried to rub the color off his face. Because they admired him, York was assigned the task of bartering with the Native Americans for food and horses.

The expedition reached the Pacific Ocean in November 1805. The group had crossed Montana, Idaho, Washington, Oregon, and North and South Dakota. After enduring a harsh winter in Washington, they returned to St. Louis, Missouri, on September 23, 1806. They had endured incredible hardships, but they brought back important information about western America.

After the expedition, Clark freed York. York traveled to Kentucky to live with his wife, who was a slave there.

Denmark Vesey (1767–1822)

Slave Revolutionary

In 1800, Denmark Vesey won 1,500 dollars in a lottery. He paid 600 dollars to buy his freedom. In 1822, he tried to gain freedom for every slave in Charleston, South Carolina. This time, he paid with his life.

After Vesey bought his freedom from the sea captain who owned him, he set up a carpentry shop. Before long, he became a wealthy man. Vesey was always outspoken about the evils of slavery. In 1821, he decided to do something about it.

Vesey and Peter Poyas decided to organize a slave revolt that would allow blacks to take over Charleston, South Carolina. Gullah Jack, an African-born magic man, was another of the leaders. Word spread quickly, and soon the group had 9,000 secret members.

The revolt was scheduled to begin on June 16, 1822. Vesey's army would move at midnight and attack several key points in the city. But a house slave betrayed their plans to the city authorities. Vesey was forced to run away from Charleston. The police found him hiding in the woods and arrested him.

At his trial, Vesey was convicted and sentenced to death. On July 2, 1822, he and five other leaders were hanged. A total of 35 black men were put to death for their parts in the revolt. They gave their lives fighting to improve the conditions of others.

Joseph Cinque (1813–1879)

Captured Slave

The only English words that Joseph Cinque knew were, "Give us free, give us free." And those were the words he spoke in a New Haven, Connecticut, courtroom in 1840. His trial was the most sensational one of its time. It became a rallying point for northern abolitionists, who were trying to end slavery in the United States.

It all started in Lomboko, Africa, in 1839. Joseph Cinque was captured by Portuguese slave traders and put aboard a ship bound for Havana, Cuba. The conditions on the ship were horrible. Half of the slaves died during the journey. Because it was illegal to import new slaves to Havana, Cinque was secretly sold to a man named Ruiz.

Cinque was put on board the Amistad, a ship bound for the Island of Principe. Desperate to escape, he pried a nail out of the ship's side and used it to unfasten the chains that bound him and the other slaves. The freed slaves sneaked onto the deck and killed the captain and the crew. Then they captured Ruiz and his partner Montes. The Africans did not know how to pilot a large ship, so they made Ruiz and Montes do the sailing.

Cinque ordered Montes to point the ship east so that the slaves could return to Africa. But Montes turned the ship northward in the middle of the night. They landed in Montauk Point on Long Island, New York. When Cinque and some other Africans went ashore to find food and water, they were arrested and charged with mutiny and murder.

The Cuban government demanded that the ship and the slaves be returned to them. American abolitionists protested, saying that Montes and Ruiz were the real criminals.

Cinque's trial was held in January 1840, in New Haven, Connecticut. The trial was featured in all the major newspapers. Yale Law School canceled classes so that its students could attend. Cinque could not speak English. He argued through an interpreter that he had been kidnapped and had a right to resist by any means necessary. The court agreed, but the decision was appealed. A higher court upheld the decision. Cinque and the other Africans were allowed to remain free.

But President Martin Van Buren wanted to please Southern slaveholders. He ordered the Justice Department to appeal the case again, this time to the Supreme Court.

At this point, former President John Quincy Adams came out of retirement to represent the Africans. Adams was almost 80 years old and nearly blind, but he was still active in the antislavery movement. After arguing before the Supreme Court for eight hours, Adams won the case.

President Martin Van Buren

John Quincy Adams

On March 9, 1841, nearly two years after he had been kidnapped, Cinque was set free. He and the other Africans returned to Sierra Leone. They were among the few slaves that were allowed their freedom in American courtrooms.

Garcia (17??–1816)

Soldier

Before Florida became a state, many slaves ran away and sought refuge there. Many runaway slaves settled among the Seminole Indian tribes. Others started small communities in the dense forests. Over 300 people of black, Seminole, and mixed descent lived in one settlement called Fort Negro. The fort was protected by black soldiers under the command of a man named Garcia.

Fort Negro was originally built by the British on the Apalachicola River, about 60 miles from Georgia. The British abandoned the fort after losing the War of 1812. Black settlers moved in, and the fort quickly became a symbol of freedom for Southern slaves. Many ran away hoping to live there.

The fort was in territory owned by Spain. But southern slaveholders were concerned that the fort posed a threat to their way of life. United States General Andrew Jackson ordered the Seventh Military to destroy Fort Negro. Attacking a fort in Spanish territory was considered an invasion of a foreign country, but Jackson ordered the attack anyway.

On the morning of July 27, 1816, a large United States military force surrounded Fort Negro. They ordered Garcia to surrender. He refused. The fort was strong and the men inside were heavily armed. The U.S. forces heated up cannonballs and fired them into the fort. One of the hot cannonballs landed in a shed full of gunpowder. It set off an explosion that was heard for miles around. The fiery blast killed or wounded almost 300 people inside the fort. Those who survived were returned to slavery. The brave commander Garcia was shot by a firing squad.

A Final Word

This book describes just a few of the many heroes who struggled against slavery. Many others also performed acts of kindness, bravery, and strength. In Africa, on the slave ships, in the markets, and on the plantations, people banded together to survive. If you want to read more about these brave men and women, the information is only as far away as your local library.

The Louisiana Purchase doubled the size of the United States overnight. At a cost of $1.80/square mile, it is considered one of the greatest land deals in history.

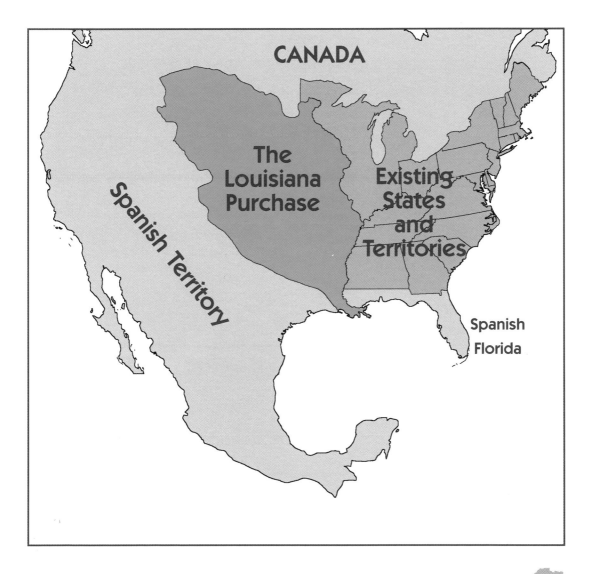

INTERNET SITES

The African-American Mosaic
http://lcweb.loc.gov/exhibits/african/afam001.html

> *This site details black history from the colonization of Liberia to Roosevelt's "new deal" in the 1930s. Browse through the pictures of historical people and documents, or see what the other links have to offer.*

African-American Odyssey–Library of Congress
http://lcweb2.loc.gov/ammem/aaohtml/

> *This Library of Congress site contains a history of blacks in America from slavery to civil rights. Check out pictures, links to other sites, and a collection of works by influential blacks in history.*

Africans In America
http://www.pbs.org/wgbh/aia/home.html

> *Relive America's journey through slavery with images, stories, documents, and narratives.*

A Slave Ship Speaks–The Wreck of the Henriette Marie
http://www.historical-museum.org/exhibits/hm/henmarie.htm

> *This site tells the story of a sunken slave ship in Florida with pictures of artifacts found on board. Take a virtual tour of the museum, or hit the links to other sites.*

GLOSSARY

Abolitionists—People who believed slavery should be illegal.

Almanac—A publication with astronomical (about the stars) and meteorological (about the weather) information arranged according to the days, weeks, and months of a given year. Almanacs also contain general information about world events and individual places.

American Colonization Society—Society formed by American slaveholders around 1810 who wanted to send free blacks back to Africa so they could not influence the slaves. The American Congress agreed with the Society and purchased a Territory in Africa which they named Liberia. Over 14,000 blacks went to Liberia by the mid 1800s. Others stayed in America to fight for the freedom of all blacks.

Amistad—A slave ship that was taken over by the slaves on board. The slaves killed all but two of the crew members, who they needed to sail the ship. The crewmen pointed the ship East and the ship landed in New York where the slaves were arrested. The slaves eventually won their freedom in court, arguing that they had been kidnapped and therefore had the right to protect themselves.

Back-To-Africa Movement—Paul Cuffe, a black shipping merchant, started this movement to form a colony in Africa where American blacks could go to live in freedom. He took the first group of people to Sierra Leone (a country in Africa) in 1815.

Battle of Bunker Hill—A Revolutionary War battle in 1775, where 1500 American soldiers held off 2500 British soldiers. The British charged up Bunker hill time after time, but the Americans fought them off. One of the top British majors, John Pitcairn, was killed at Bunker Hill when he thought the British had won. As Pitcairn proclaimed victory Peter Salem, a black American soldier, shot him in the chest. His loss was a tremendous blow to the British, and Salem became a hero.

Boston Massacre—The start of events that triggered the American Revolution. In 1770, when the British still controlled America, a group of American protesters were gathered in Boston Commons taunting a small group of British soldiers. One of the soldiers struck a small boy and the crowd pelted him with snowballs. More soldiers joined the group with their weapons pointed at the crowd. Crispus Attucks, a black man, charged forward calling on the rest of the crowd to follow. The soldiers opened fire and killed five men, including Attucks.

Cotton Gin—Invented by Eli Whitney in 1793, the cotton gin was a machine that separated sticky cotton seeds from the fibers. This invention made it possible for slaves to produce 50 times as much cotton as they could separating the seeds by hand. The cotton gin was one of the greatest inventions of its time.

Dialect—A variation of a language with different vocabulary, grammar, and pronunciation than other varieties of the same language.

Expedition—A journey taken for a specific purpose, like exploring an unknown territory, or searching for a new territory.

Fort Negro—An old Fort in the Spanish territory of Florida originally built by the British that was settled by blacks, Seminole Indians, and people of mixed race. The fort was a symbol of freedom for Southern blacks, and many slaves ran away hoping to live there. The United States army attacked the fort in 1816 because they considered it a threat to the Southern way of life. The fort was destroyed, and those who survived were returned to slavery.

Hoecake—A cornmeal cake that was heated over an open fire on a gardening hoe. Hoecake was a main meal for many slaves in the South.

Louisiana Purchase—The acquisition of 875,000 square miles of unexplored territory from the Mississippi River to the Rocky Mountains. This territory, purchased by President Thomas Jefferson from the French in 1803, doubled the size of the United States.

Plantations—Large estates in the South that raised crops, usually tobacco or cotton, with slave labor. Plantations typically had enormous houses and hundreds of acres of land with stables, smokehouses, bake houses, dairies, schoolhouses, and slave quarters, making them mostly self-sufficient.

Slave Auction—Places where plantation owners and other whites gathered to view and purchase slaves just arriving from Africa.

Slavery—The concept of owning people as property to do work for the owner. Slaves were regarded as property and not given even the basic rights of other human beings.

Slave Trade—The buying and selling of blacks for profit prior to the American Civil War. The slave trade was responsible for taking about 10 million blacks from Africa to work on American farms and plantations.

INDEX